Liberation:

The 20 Year Journey It Took To Heal My Soul

A'Kayla Harris

Cover design by A'Kayla Harris

For information to book an event and all other inquiries contact publisher via email

akaylaharrisent@gmail.com

Manufactured in the United States

ISBN: 0692361596
ISBN-13: 978-0692361597

DEDICATION

For my grandmother Lois Jean McCollum whose prayers still hold it all together today…

TABLE OF CONTENTS

ACKNOWLEDGMENTS

To my creator, thank You. There were points when I questioned Your vision for my life, and still….through it all, it's happening. You began this work in a 17 year old kid by way of a prophecy, and You have seen me through it every step of the way. I owe You my life.

To my mother and father who allowed me to tell this truth so fearlessly and with more support than I could've hoped for…I love you both to the ends of the world. Thank you for the gift of life.

To my loving God-mother Ayana Chism, you're awesome! You've never made me feel uncomfortable about being a mess. Your love, support and guidance have carried me through the worst of times.

To my new favorite cousin, Erin Mercer, Ms. McCall, Dr. Dilworth, and Dr. Fridge (my professors and mentors) thank you guys for gently guiding me along the way to produce this work and supporting my efforts.

To Dr. Evans in the "towers" of THEE Jackson State University, I still don't know how you do what you do for me what button you press, but thank you!

To the friends and family that previewed this book and gave me constructive feedback, thank you from the bottom of my heart.

Introduction

Welcome to my mind, but not really, I'm nervous…but you gotta let me be awkward cause this is my book.

First of all you'll have to focus when I'm speaking. I'm scatterbrained but if you pay close attention and read carefully everything will make sense. I say exactly what I feel the moment I feel it. I like ellipses (…) so you'll see them often. Sprinkled throughout this book are pieces of poetry and letters I wrote over a span of about 5 years. You'll know when a piece starts and ends because it will be separated from the rest of the story and dated.

As a budding author I often questioned whether or not I was being too "raw" for people to relate to my work but I noticed that when I compromised, it became someone else's story. I hope you welcome all of my scattered pieces with open hearts and minds. I'll talk to you often throughout the book because although I was an English major at my prior university, I've never done well with staying in the proper tense. For your sake, after the first few pages of this book I'll begin to list things chronologically although that's not how the thoughts came to me. You're welcome. Carry on

There's a culture I like to call "purity and perfection" that pressures women from birth to submit to societal expectations. Women are supposed to be polite, graceful, gentle, and speak in monotone voices so they don't offend people. I often read articles about women who have faced great difficulty and opposition to reach a certain point in their careers. Would you like to know how they're described? As poised and graceful. On the flipside male figures within the same predicaments are described by writers as tough, powerful and resilient. I've always struggled balancing what was expected of me, with who I really am. I am rough. I am bold and I am unapologetic. I've always had a good idea of the type of person I wanted to be but after my thoughts had been gentrified through the "purity and perfection" process I was confused. Everyone wants you to just "be yourself" until who you are begins offends them. Whenever I was direct about what I thought I was a labeled as an individual with a bad attitude. When I was meek and submissive I was a door mat. How can you express yourself when every part of your creative process has to go through the scrutiny of what people will think? You don't realize how detrimental your thought process is until you see people take their lives and harm others all because of what lives inside their heads. I had to fight my thoughts and find a sense of personal conviction – sometimes beyond human understanding – that allowed me to finally be an *individual.*

What I've learned is that as long as you put who you are into the world and work really hard at perfecting your talent everything that is attracted to whatever you're doing – will come. This law of attraction is not superstition or voodoo but rather a matter of common sense. It's simply advertising whatever you please about yourself to get your desired outcome. That's all every profession is, a bunch of people who found out what they were good at and capitalized off their natural abilities. First, you've got to figure out why in the world you're here. That task may be easier for some than others. We've all been brought up within different religions, cultures, and social norms. When we are young, that's what shapes who we are and how we feel about ourselves and others. As we grow we begin to formulate our own thoughts and find out some of what was engrained in us is as children hardly matters to us at all, or just isn't true.

Most of who I am today is the result of my "liberation" process. I've spent countless hours becoming a student of life. I believe the learning process never ends. Every time Vincent Van Gogh felt like he had mastered a particular painting technique he would abandon it, and learn a new one all over again. These past few months I have learned anything I could from anyone I came into contact with. On this journey I had to be trained to love like God loves. When you love like He does there is no room for resentment and condemnation of your bother. You stop being so desperate to be understood and learn how to be understanding. You forget what people owe you and begin to brainstorm about what you have to add to society. Before you reach this point there must be awakening that happens. Most people don't feel the chains until it's time to move. When you become "aware" you'll see that some of the things your mother told you weren't right, half the authors of your school textbooks hid the important stuff and that sometimes even our leaders don't have all the answers. When you get there you'll just want to know what to believe in and what to let go of.

....But first, you must break away from whatever set of rules you've lived by your entire life.

2 Peter 2:19 (kjv)

"While they promise them liberty, they themselves are the servants of corruption: for of whom a man is overcome, of the same is he brought in bondage."

The Rules **10/12/09**

I am full of things I still don't
understand about myself.

I've made so many decisions I
regret that I'd rather consciously
fall into the same mess than
venture into new territory and
wear
yet
another
badge of defeat.

The consequences a dreamer must
face lie between the dream and
what's visible.

Who will be brave enough to
believe in the things they can't
see?

Rejection still sits like a lump in
my throat.

I've been offered the world and
denied the art of true expression.

You've got to cross your legs like
this, or dress like that to taste
these privileges.

You have adhere to a secret
system of rules to move up or be
Black,
ugly,
poor,
and die.

The Breaking Point

I lost my mind in my car yesterday. I was crying so hard that I had to pull over and ask God for strength to make it home.

...but I lost myself a long time ago. I decided to spend a week of my winter break in Jackson, TN and it flipped my entire life upside down. It also helped me understand why it was so urgent to release this book. I thought about killing myself on the car ride back to Mississippi yesterday. It wasn't the first time that I'd visualized myself in my casket or who would mourn at my funeral and who wouldn't bother to come at all. I used to be one of those people who couldn't fathom one scenario horrible enough to make me want to kill myself until…life happened.

I got horribly drunk Christmas eve and woke up in a daze Christmas morning. I spent the rest of the day with a good friends family. I hated the thought of having to introduce myself to everyone in the room on Christmas day. I thought holidays were for family, familiarity, and fun so I faked all of those things yesterday. The day after Christmas I left Tennessee without saying goodbye to anyone but my mother. I just woke up over my friend's house, picked up my Wal-Mart bag of clothes and rode out. They say you have fifteen seconds to entertain or grab a reader's attention before they put your book down. This book was not created on the premises of entertaining you. Everything I say is my truth, even the ugly things about myself that I've never admitted to anyone. I know fancy words, and I'm pretty good at using them correctly...but again, I'm not trying to impress you. I need the high school dropouts, the collegiates on the brink of suicide, and adults wandering aimlessly throughout life to understand this. Even if you don't fit any of those categories I hope you haven't made up in your mind you don't need to read this book, if so, your loss.

Before you continue reading... this is the only warning you'll get. Absolutely nothing is off limits here. There is no such this as being discrete and transparent in *my* world simultaneously. The only thing I've decided not to do is include anyone's real name that could potentially be ostracized, or get their feelings hurt. I'm not looking to get an emotional response out of you either, but rather motivate you enough to follow your dreams. This book is to save someone's life. That's probably as plain as I can make it. Might be yours, or whomever you decide to hand it to. This is my truth and I hope it helps you on your own journey of healing and self-discovery. When you reach your breaking point with a certain situation it'll hit you hard. Don't give in. Don't fold up. The most crucial thing to remember is that someway, somehow you will survive. It's mandatory that you cut off anything in your space that sucks life from you. It doesn't matter how big or small, how long you've known a person, or how familiar you are with the territory. If it is draining you, it **must** leave.

Somebody is going to need to hear about how you made it.

Read that last sentence aloud until it resonates with your soul. We all have been through something, are currently going through something, or have another storm up ahead. What if I told you whatever you're going through presently was specifically designed for you to be able to encourage someone else? How would you look at your struggles if you knew your story could save someone's life one day? Become the ambassador of your pain and realize that you're paying a heavy price because you've got a heavy calling.

One of my goals is to help redesign the way you think about tough situations in your life. I've spent the last two years of my life recovering from my childhood, only to find that I'm not the only nutcase, just one of the only ones willing to tell their story. You may not have known you that you were on a path, but the moment you began reading this book you started walking with me. Let's get free together.

Dealing With It (Whatever Your "it" may be)

I've been molested three times. I'll only list one instance in this book for the sake of me not having to relive each time. I felt the same emotions every time, and I always found a way to make it my fault. The first time was in a room of a house me and my mother lived in around the age of 5 or 6. We we're staying with an elderly church member until my mom could get her own apartment. I remember being downstairs playing with my toy vanity (you know the ones with the cool fake makeup and lip gloss included?) and the darker one of the elderly woman's granddaughters, who were both considerably older than myself, called me upstairs. They usually didn't yell my name like she did unless I was getting on their nerves or I'd done something wrong. I rushed upstairs to be met with a calm countenance, which was weird. She stared at me for minute and then told me to go to her room. I did as I was ordered, although I was still confused.

After I sat on the bed for a minute, she finally came in and closed and locked the door behind her. My mother was at work and she entrusted her to take care of me while she was gone. I asked her why she called me upstairs, partially apologizing (just in case I'd messed up anything that I'd forgotten about) and she told me that I hadn't. By this point I'm genuinely curious as to what she wants from me. I remember her turning on the radio and then ordering me to pull down my pants and my favorite power puff girl panties. She then directed me to the bed. I started to cry, and she told me to shut up and that if I ever told anyone she would kill me. So I cried silently. She opened my little legs and violated me repeatedly, sometimes with her hand, sometimes with her mouth, and sometimes with an object. It hurt so badly, but I remember telling myself that I had to be brave. I put my hand over my mouth, and closed my eyes tightly and tried to think about my grandmother. After she was done, she told me I needed to return the "favor", and I did. Except, I had no idea what I was doing and she got so frustrated with me that she ended up just telling me to go back downstairs. I felt sick. I have tried to suppress this memory since it happened, thinking I could make it go away…but I can't. I had good intentions and no matter how perverted she was I still just wanted to oblige and make her happy. That might have actually been my biggest problem as a child that transferred into adulthood, wanting to please everyone. My heart was so pure and content with hurting for the sake of others happiness.

When it was all over, I wanted to run out of the house as far as possible and just be with my grandma one more time. She died the year before that happened to me though, so in my six year old mind...nobody could know. Everyone would think I was lying. I carried the weight of the shame as if I'd willingly invited her into my space.

It's funny how I remember everything surrounding the event and my molester has probably forgotten. She was a teenager at the time and I'm not sure if she was curious or really had devious intentions to hurt me, but I can remember never being angry with her. I was scared of her, but never felt like she *meant* to hurt me. I've always been the type of person who tries understand the thought process of "bad" people rather than condemn them.

Some type of way I ended up feeling sorry for her. There's an African proverb I committed to memory that states "the axe forgets, but the tree remembers." Those who have cut us rarely have to deal with the ramifications of the act they committed against us, while we spend our entire lives trying to forget it. I'm now at an age of understanding where I realize what happened to me wasn't my fault, but I still do struggle with why it happened in the first place. What went wrong in her life that caused the spirit of perversion to fall upon her so heavily? Had someone done the same to her?

The crazy thing about it all is that I recognize my eyes in other children who have been victimized. I'm familiar with those mannerisms, and sometimes even the promiscuous nature that ensues. This book is for you. You can be a 30-year-old man or woman, and still approach the thing that hurt you as if you were a child again. A lot of us never deal with it. We suppress it until it's almost as if it didn't happen at all. That tactic turned out to be explosive for me. When I finally sat down to write this book all those memories came pouring in at once. Here I was, 20 years old crying like I was six again, balled up in a fetal position. I cried and held myself until God reminded me that I wasn't in danger anymore.

I *had* to deal with it though...I had to get to a point where the fear of re-opening those memories was not greater than the benefits of healing my heart. It will hurt, most definitely, but sometimes you just gotta take care of you. You owe it to yourself to **take care of you.** You don't have to justify self-care. You don't have to wait until a disaster happens in your life to be nice to yourself. Taking care of ourselves means different things for different people. For me it was writing letters to my molesters that I never sent. I told them about how much it hurt, and how my private parts were puffy and sore afterwards. I spoke to them about how my self worth plummeted afterwards, how it affected the way I dealt with people, and my social awkwardness. The last thing I mentioned was that even though they never acknowledged it and I'd probably never receive an apology… I forgave them.

Sometimes you have to re-invent what closure means to you, or forever think someone owes you something. No one owes you consistency, time, kindness or effort. The quicker you realize most people only give based off of what they receive, the better. I forced myself to release any of the power they still held over my life. I cannot describe in words alone how redeeming that was for me. To realize that regardless to what happened to me that I was not "damaged goods". I'm still precious, I still matter, and I'm whole again. I learned how not to make a lifetime out of a singular moment that cut me.

Anytime I was scared, or nervous I thought about my grandmother and I think it's because how she made me feel when I was around her…all loved, and safe in her arms. That was the second time I'd been scared half to death in that house. The first time is half comical and borderline abuse, just depends on what you're into. The girls told me that they were about to walk to the store and to make sure I didn't answer the door for anyone. I took this responsibility seriously. After all, what other six year old got stay at home alone? (that was soooo dope to me in my head) I would find out why people don't leave six year olds home alone within the next thirty minutes though.

I moved about the house as normal cutting on my favorite cartoons in the living room, eating Hallelujah Night (Halloween) candy my mother had hidden from me and I even contemplated making me a peanut butter and jelly sandwich with one of the sharp knives I wasn't supposed to touch, cause I could do that. The next thing I remember is someone beating really hard on the living room window. I ran as quickly as I could to the back of the house and hid under the bed in the room adjacent to me and my mother's (we shared a room). "Whoever" was banging on the living room window came to the back and did the same thing. I can remember being so scared I peed on myself a little bit. I cried so hard I got a fever. They finally busted through the back door in the elderly woman's room (where I was hiding) and I immediately stopped crying, and breathing too. I was under the impression this was a real house intrusion and I refused to give myself up for sacrifice. Soon after hearing the voices of the people who busted in, I realized it was the girl's voices. After a few minutes of them walking through the house without finding me, the joke was on them. The girls thought I'd really left the house. Their laughs soon turned into an argument over whose terrible idea it was to leave me at the house by myself in the first place. I finally came from under the bed eyes red, with a burning headache and soaked panties laughing hysterically at them. They'd let a six year old beat them at their own game. They didn't find it as funny as I did though so I was cursed out and forced to take a nap. It didn't matter though, because they'd still been outsmarted.

Surprisingly something beautiful did come out of that situation. When I was under that bed scared for my life, I said my first prayer without the help of my grandmother. She's the one that taught me how to pray. She used to make me kneel next to her every night and repeat after her, and tell God what I was thankful for. Sometimes my prayers were rather long when I listed everyone I wanted God to bless but she never cut me off or got frustrated with me. I'm not even sure she knew how beneficial that practice would be for me as I got older.

Genesis 50:20 (niv)

"You intended to harm me, but God intended it for good to accomplish what is now being done, the saving of many lives."

Humble Beginnings

Elementary school was an absolute breeze for me. My mother had been correcting my grammar and making me read far before I ever started grade school. The only issue my teachers had with me was that there was literally no filter from my mind to mouth. If I thought it, I said it. When I was in the third grade my social studies teacher was attempting to teach the class about African slavery and its connection to the civil rights movement…as honestly as she could. She informed us that some of our grandparents may remember different parts of the movement and gave us an assignment to go ask them about their experience and/or involvement during that era. I was so upset that no one had ever told me all these things before about *my* people and I was seriously thinking about letting all my white friends go at recess time. I didn't quite grasp the time difference that stood between myself and the civil rights movement, and then her throwing the assignment in that included my grandmamma didn't make it any better.

I had to get some type of understanding of what was going on. I raised my hand, and when she called on me I said vindictively, "You mean to tell me, YALL (she was white) put MY grandma in chains and then made it hard for her to get a job?" I wish I could've taken a picture of her face. That was the first time I seen anyone turn the shade of red she did. She called my mother and told her she didn't know how to answer my questions and that I was putting negative connotations in the other children's minds. Luckily, my mother understood the value of a child's inquisitiveness and told me to never stop asking questions. I didn't. I got a few calls home a year and it was the always the same thing, not disciplinary, but that I wanted to know "too much" which made me a distraction. Except for that one time I got caught stealing the snacks out of everyone's lunches and then selling them on the bus…but that's another story for another day. That my friends, is a story of entrepreneurship.

I honestly don't remember much about Beloit, Wisconsin but a whole lotta church. My mother and I were up at the church or in somebody's rehearsal almost every day for something. My mother was the drummer for our church, helped direct the praise team, and was a praise dancer all in one. I just remember feeling talentless. I was rhythm less, couldn't hold a tune, or dance. The only thing I knew for sure I was good at was talking and getting on everyone's nerves. As much as I grew to hate church, bible studies, revivals, and concerts (we attended them ALL) I do remember the day things got really serious for me at church.

By serious, I mean, my first visitation of the Holy Spirit...Holy Ghost if you're Baptist. I was eight, and up until then I really didn't think all the falling out folks did was necessary. I usually laughed at all the ridiculousness that surrounded me. My Sundays consisted of one of the mother's skirts falling down while she was givin' Him glory, my chunky auntie pooting wayyy too loud during morning prayer and me embarrassing a cross eyed man because I couldn't tell if he was trying to get my attention, or one of my cousins.

One day a little bald bishop from somewhere down south came through my church. I can't remember his name for the life of me, but I remember his face perfectly, and my God he was

OILY! (let me break it down for the slow saints…oily is a term used to identify with someone or something that is anointed, powerful, and impactful) I knew he was a big deal from the way he walked in with his long red robe, armor bearer and three deacons in perfect formation behind him. He articulated every word he spoke to the tee and added his own southern twang on top of it. I followed his whole sermon, and felt convicted (about ripping up my pink slip from school) to walk to the altar for prayer.

I was the last person he laid hands on and he immediately started prophesying over my life. All the adults around me we're crying and speaking in tongues. I didn't feel anything in particular until I decided to lift my hands, and then, like a ton of bricks I felt His presence. I fell to my knees and cried uncontrollably. This was God, and there was no denying it. This time I wasn't practicing my shout, I wasn't faking my tears, I couldn't stop my feet from moving and I didn't care what my friends in the pews thought of me. My aunt had to carry me to the back of the church to the day care area and lay me on a couch because even after worship service had ended, I was still on the altar. I'd given every ounce of myself to God. That was one of the most beautiful experiences of my life. If you've never had the opportunity to feel monogamous with whomever you consider a "divine" being…try it. My belief in God is the only thing that has kept me sane and alive. Whoever you are, whatever your belief system, and even if you don't have one at all...find what makes you happy to be alive, and stay close to it.

In Wisconsin my mother and I never lived anywhere really fancy but I don't recall us ever being anywhere run down either. She was perfect to me, and spoiled me absolutely rotten. All I had to do was name it and it was mine. It was important to her that I didn't become braggadocios about the benefits of being an only child. She was mine, and I was hers and there was nothing that could come between that.

Sometimes in the middle of the night I could feel her pull my cover up to tuck me in and then kiss me on the forehead or cheek. It was like a gentle reminder that I would always be the apple of her eye. We had amazing movie nights in the basement of our first house. She would order us calzones (ham and cheese for me, and pepperoni and mushrooms for herself) and let me stay up until I was falling over. On most Christmases I wouldn't get around to playing with all the toys she'd gotten me until the next week or so. Those are some of the best days I remember having with my mother. She did the best she could with what she had and it was more than I could've ever asked for. Looking back, the material things didn't come close to the intimate time we spent together bonding, I'd give anything to have that back. Any time we struggled I barely noticed. She always told me the big things were for her to worry about. She carried her burdens so well that I didn't realize she had any.

Life In Michigan

At nine, my mother asked me if I wanted to move to Lansing, Michigan and I responded, "sure, why not?!" It really didn't matter what my response to the question was, we were moving regardless. I'm not sure what her intentions for moving to Lansing were besides the big lump sum of money that she would receive once we arrived. I don't think I was figured into the equation at all. A few months after we moved is when I first realized being away from everything I was familiar with would not be as easy as I initially thought.

One day I was casually taking out the trash and doing some kind of stupid dance move all at the same time. When you're an only child acting stupid is naturally your entertainment. As I was swinging the trash bag back and forth, unknowingly with broken alcohol bottles in the bottom, and I ended up slicing my ankle to the white meat. The thing about deep cuts is that they don't initially bleed, and sometimes they don't even hurt because of all the adrenaline that rushes to the wound. I threw the trash into the dumpster of our upscale apartments and walked all the way back to our building. It seems as soon as I stepped foot in our apartment my sock filled with blood and a sharp pain shot up my leg. I didn't even know I'd cut myself. My mother picked me up and put me on the bathroom counter and she and my aunt's best friend tried to rinse my wound with cool water and bandage it up. They soon realized a band-aid would not suffice, because anything they put on it I bled right through. My mom ended up taking me to the emergency room so I could get stitched up.

Thought Provoking Moment Time

How many of us have tried to put Band-Aids on spiritual wounds that called for a gauze pad or surgery? When we play the role of Creator we usually end up with something more infectious and painful than what we began with. I pray you know the difference between what is mendable, and those things that are not.

Ok, now back to the story…

A nice, slim white lady led us to the room where my procedure would take place and helped me get onto the cold bed/long sheet of construction paper that's always on hospital beds. I sat there for a while talking casually with my mom about the first time I had to get stitches and how she left me in the room with one of my aunts because she couldn't stand to see me cry. I told her she would have to stay this time because there was no one else there to stay with me, and I made fun of her about chickening out the first time. A little while before the nurse came back in the midst of our jokes my mom slowed the pace of her laugh, looked at me and said, "Kayla what would you say if I told you I was gay?" I laughed so hard tears started to form in the corners of my eyes because I knew this *had* to be a joke. I knew this was the most ridiculous, absurd scenarios she could think of…but it wasn't. She stopped laughing all together and said, "Kayla, I'm gay." Again, I didn't know how to respond…I just said "ok, mom", surrendering all of my true feelings to comfort her. I was confused. Her timing couldn't have been more horrible.

When the doctor came in to stitch up my ankle, again, my mother told me she would have to step out the room. I was really sad until the nurse came in and offered to hold my hand throughout the entire procedure. I still couldn't understand my mother's reasoning behind not being available when I needed her, because "she didn't like to see me in pain." She didn't know the nurse would offer to stay by my side but she knew I was scared, and that I freaked out around needles. I told her she didn't even have to look at my ankle being worked on, just be there so I wouldn't have to be alone. I thought she should've swallowed her fear to comfort mine, but instead it was the other way around. I reasoned with myself that my physical pain was of lesser value than what my mother felt emotionally when she seen me lying there, and that I was stronger than she was and I could handle being alone. While the doctor was working I couldn't think about anything but what my mother had just told me. I tried to digest it, and figure out how we were going to be able to live a normal life from that point forward. I remember my thoughts moving at the speed of lightning on that hospital bed. I was going in and out of my "thinking space" back to the realization that there was a needle penetrating my skin over and over again.

After the doctor finished stitching me up and I picked out what I thought was a satisfactory sticker for the eight stitches I'd just had to endure, we we're on our way out of the hospital. The only thing my nine year old self could figure up to say to my mother was, "Thanks mom, a lot of parents wouldn't have told their children something like that." This is was the first actual turning point in my life. I was nine. I didn't know what the heck a lot of parents would or wouldn't have told their children. I was just trying to make sure my mother didn't think I was uncomfortable with her or loved her any less. I had everything confused. Loving someone has everything to do with being able to be as honest as possible and still knowing that no matter how I feel, I *still* love you.

The next couple of years of my life were complex and frustrating. Up until that point I had been virtually raised in church. I couldn't understand how my mother could just dispose a system of beliefs as easily as she did. Although I hated church, I loved dressing up and getting my hair done for service and wondering what we would eat afterwards. I loved God. My little relationship with Him was in its early stages but my prayer life was like that of a woman who had become well adjusted to life's disappointments. For about the first 5 months or so in Lansing I only saw my mother on the ride to and from overnight care during the week.

Moms worked the night shift so in the mornings she would wake me up, get me in the shower and then on my way to school. After school, I would walk home and my things would already be packed and ready to go. I finally told my mother that only the first floor of the house/daycare she would take me to was kid friendly. I slept on a single mattress in one of the upstairs bedrooms with only a fan and TV. I usually just used my jacket to cover me at night because everything they owned reeked of cat pee. The owners had 5 or so cats that roamed around the house at any given time. I begged my mom to let me just stay home alone. I figured anything was better than that, and she was tired of paying them a grip every week anyways. I'd convinced her that Melody and Harmony's (our neighbors) mom let them stay home and that we were pretty close in age. She finally obliged to my request, though reluctantly.

The first time I wanted to kill myself was in the fourth grade while attending El Hajj Malik El Shabazz Academy located in Lansing. If you're not familiar with black history at all, this is the name Malcolm Little acquired after returning from his pilgrimage in Mecca, which he later changed to the infamous "X". I loved how intermingled black history was in the curriculum at Shabazz academy. Most of the teachers were black, and we used to have little programs for black history with food, native music and dances once a month. I was still advanced for my age and I still talked way too much, but my favorite teacher had a remedy for that. Unknowingly, at first, he'd been giving me extra worksheets with my assignments because I finished so quickly. Talk about constructive teaching methods! Instead of complaining to my mother that I talked too much, he pushed me harder than the other kids. Mr. McCants did an amazing job dealing with me. He didn't take on the saturated, top-down approach so many parents and instructors use today. Kids that act the way I did today usually get prescribed some sort of dose of Adderall, or Ritalin but luckily tough love was enough for me. He would take me out of the class and talk to me for a few moments and I'd be fine.

He dealt with me like he loved me and actually cared about what became of me.

I do remember the one time he sent me to the office though; I had vandalized a wall on the stairwell to my classroom and was caught on camera doing it. To this day I don't know why I wrote what I wrote on that wall. It was something around the lines of "Your mama is a b****." Maybe it was because of all the criticism I received the day before from my mother's parent-teacher conference attire. She decided it was fitting to wear baggy jeans and some sort of oversized men's brand t-shirt up to my school. I was honestly cool with what she had on… until all the whispers that "Kayla's mom was a dike, and looked like a man" started floating around. In my child-like thoughts my mother couldn't get anything right. First she took me away from all my family and friends in my hometown, and now she chooses to embarrass me in front of my new ones? My frustration with her was growing quickly and I had absolutely no one to talk to about it. She'd also recently lost her job at General Motors and started working at a bread store. She'd eventually lose her car too so we were catching rides everywhere for a little minute. Along with all of that, I'd lost the only thing I thought could possibly comfort me, which was church. I don't remember attending one service the entire three years we lived in Lansing. So the day after she came up to my school, with all my combined frustrations, I acted out.

As I walked to the office, via the orders of Mr. McCants, for what I thought would be a lengthy suspension I tried to think of a lie that would keep me in school. I had nothing. I was just frustrated with life. Before my principal Dr. Cain called my mother he asked me why I did it, and I burst into tears. I honestly couldn't even form the words to tell him all that was going on in my little life… about all the women entering and exiting our small apartment, about my mother leaving me to attend night clubs with her friends, and me feeling abandoned. He decided to extend grace instead of suspend me. I vividly remember Dr. Cain picking me up from the chair I was sitting in and giving me a hug. He let me explain everything that I'd held in for the past five months and opened up about his family a bit. Here was a man who could've been fired for touching me alone, who pushed everything to the side to listen to me. Not only was I relieved he decided not to call my mother, but he also gave me sound advice that I'll never forget. He said jokingly, "you write well for your age, whenever you're feeling how you felt today from now on I want you to write it down in a journal. You can cuss there. There are no rules or anyone to tell you how you should feel there." From that point on, that's exactly what I did. By the time I reached high school I had written volumes of poetry and at least two or three books over my life already, I just didn't know it.

The Move Back to Tennessee

Life in Michigan ended as quickly as it had begun. After my mother lost pretty much everything there I guess she figured it was time for a scene change. The fact that my aunt was sick helped seal the deal on the move back to Jackson, Tennessee. For the first few months we lived with my aunt Greta. That was an experience within itself. She's a different type of woman and what I mean by different is that you'd honestly just have to meet her to know what I'm talking about. Nevertheless, I was grateful for her generosity until my mother and I got a place on our own. The duplex we moved into in hillcrest circle was kind of creepy and looked like a cabin on the inside because everything was wooden, but I was just excited about having my own room and space again. I'm guessing my mother had a hard time finding work in Tennessee so she just ended up working at a local gas station with my aunt Emonda. I couldn't understand that, I'd always looked at my mother as the most intelligent, beautiful, artistic woman in the world…I wondered how she would use all her talents at a gas station. That's just the way life goes sometimes I guess. After a few months of living in our new duplex my mother met a woman I'll call "Shonda" for the sake of her privacy. After what seemed to be about five visits, we we're packing up and moving into her three bedroom apartment with her five children.

I felt like I was fighting for my life daily. I woke up heavy, and went to bed heavy. By this time I'd learn how to become a recluse. I just longed to be alone whenever I was around anyone. I can remember there being a noticeable difference in the way she treated me in comparison to her own children. The best way to describe my experience in Shonda's home was pure hell and even that may very well be an understatement. My mother and she got in a physical altercation one day and she broke my mother's glasses. I stood in the doorway and watched the entire thing. I'd never seen my mother so angry…and then punked out so quickly. It's like she was afraid to make her too upset because she feared we could be homeless at any minute. I watched Shonda beat and kick her pregnant daughter down the steps of the apartment in front of everyone. I slept on the floor the first three months we lived there partially hoping we would eventually move out and in part because I didn't know the woman's daughters well enough to sleep in the same bed with them. My mother had already hung up her clothes, and had a comfortable living space, and bed might I add. I was still searching through 3 bins looking for my clothes every morning. I believe this is when I actually started losing hope. I really thought nothing would ever get better for my mother and I. I'd made up in my mind she would always be in toxic relationships and how I felt about them would never matter. I tried to reach out a few times to people, but I couldn't even begin to explain what I was feeling inside.

I often heard the oldest sister having sex in the room next door, and watched her son roll and sell weed like it was a part of his religion. The youngest daughter was raped at gunpoint at the dumpster by our neighbor's older brother who had been recently released from prison. I was supposed to have been out there with her that night but I made a fuss because I'd already washed the dishes alone. I heard my mother and Shonda turn up the music when they we're having sex in the room next to me, but nothing they did could drown out the screams and noises I heard on that top bunk. I would get nauseous and head to the bathroom every time. I got so used to the dysfunctional nature of that house that it almost became normal.

Many people don't make it out of toxic households relatively unscathed. If you're like myself there's a few questions you need to ask yourself before the healing process begins.

1. What situations have you been placed in where you were left without any control?
2. How did the turmoil around you shape who you are today?
3. Are you addicted to dysfunction/drama? and the attention you receive from it?

A trend I've noticed amongst people who come from torn homes is the inability to accept genuine love. To them everybody has an angle or expects something out of them because that's the type of people they're used to being around. Don't shut people out who want to be there for you. It's rare to find people that will stick around through your shenanigans and not expect anything of you. Embrace them, they're God-sent. Sometimes we're so afraid of something real leaving our grasp that we push away anything and anyone that feels too good to be true. The people around you may not understand it…but I do, and I got you.

All I'm asking you to do is to love like you've never been hurt before. What if God loved you based off your actions toward Him? A lot of us would be in absolute despair if that was the case, myself included. Swallow people whole that you care about with your love. Make your love inescapable so that even after people leave your presence they still have a little bit of you….on them. Even if your like me and you've tried it all with all the wrong people, try again. Value yourself enough to step outside of what your used to. Better to accidently find the real deal, than to have not tried at all.

Mama's Baby

My relationship with my mother has always been on the most basic of terms. I've never gone a day hungry or unclothed. For that, I'm grateful but there's so much more to parenting and loving a child than making sure they have the essentials. I suppose, she didn't really understand how to be affectionate because as the older generation says, "the similac was still on her breath" when she had me.

I like to think my physical proportions were more meaningful than my actual birthday. I was born in Beloit, Wisconsin at Beloit Memorial Hospital weighing seven pounds, seven ounces. The number seven has many meanings but the one I've attached myself to is that of completion. I was born completely oblivious, and innocent as to what type of life awaited me and my nineteen year old mother. I used to wonder what would have happened had I been born to another woman. A woman that had more money, more experience, and one that was more prepared for a child. I would soon snap out of this day dream and just thank God I wasn't aborted. I watched a video in which an "underground" surgeon removed a four to five month old fetus and I seen its and hands and feet twitching and it's features all bloody. At least I wasn't that child. Right?

The crazy thing about this seven number, as it pertains to my life, is the fact that my mother and my father were born at the exact same weight that I was. This could be some type of coincidence but I honestly believe it's a divine encounter. I'm not into numerology but the odds of that happening are quite rare I'm certain. Plus whenever there is room for me to think I'm special, I will. You can laugh here…I know I'm crazy.

As far back as I can remember there has always been something disconnected between she and I. Around the age of understanding when I really began to form my own opinions and connect the dots for myself she had already detached herself from everything we were familiar with in Wisconsin. She was completely submerged into the freedom the lifestyle she was living in Lansing permitted. She barely noticed I was falling apart. As I grew I became more and more confused as to what I was here to do. I started wearing clothes out of the boy's section and preferring jerseys, Tracy McGrady's, and cargos over anything pink or associated with girls. I thought that in order to please her.

My mother was my best friend, just the kind that you can't really tell any of your secrets or opinions to in fear that you'll hurt their feelings. I watched her every move. I can remember her thinking I was oblivious to everything. When the reality was… I stumbled across the dildo in the black bag in the bottom drawer of her dresser when she told me to go get her a pair of socks, I knew she was sleeping with the older man that used to come occasionally come pick us up, I'd seen the naked photographs a woman mailed/gave to her, and I stumbled across a tape of her masturbating when I was only trying to watch my old basketball games from boys and girls club.

These are amongst the things I never let her know. I can remember being disgusted with her some days and saying nothing. I just cried, prayed about it, and wrote in my journal every night. The worse part of it all was her continuously trying to introduce me to women and get me to open up. I was much smarter than her in that area though, I learned how to "fake" like them, and say whatever I needed to get new shoes or an outfit out of 'em before their time expired. The range of women my mother dated went from a deaf lady from California, a fat woman in Texas, a woman with a big booty and no brains from Atlanta, a chick still getting abused by her ex boyfriend, a girl a few years older than me from the hood, to a nurse practitioner.

To me she was *thee* definition of a playa, I don't think she had a type. These weren't the only ones either, just the most notable. I never cared for any of them. Dr. Phil said something on his show about your children knowing before you do if a person is decent, or has pure intentions with you. I'm not sure if it's true or not, but every single time I've been correct in my assumptions. These fly-bys she did never lasted long. I've noticed the longer she plays house with the woman, the more toxic the relationship gets. I was mute from 06' to 09' toward my mother. Not literally of course…but I only spoke to her on the need to know basis. I went through a period where I absolutely hated her, and everything she stood for. I told her she wasn't a good mother. She could have company and I would come in our duplex and walk directly pass her and her company and go straight to my room. I spent so much time in my room throughout my preteen years I almost forgot what the rest of the house looked like. I can only categorize different periods of my mothers and I relationship by whether or not she was involved with a woman or not. That determined how much she talked to me and how much time we spent together. When she was with someone I hardly wanted to be seen in public with her and the individual. I don't think she understood how much shame aroused in me… for her. I felt like she continually made a fool out of herself and because I wasn't old enough to get emancipated, I just had to sit back and be drug along for the ride… and drag me she did. Her relationships have always had priority in her life.

I've tried to reach her through a thousand letters, talks, and long text messages. Seems like nothing I did could have made her see herself as I did. It seems like she just took whatever people gave her when it came to her heart. Unfortunately every time she hurt…so did I. I've been bleeding out for years for her while trying to patch her heart. I can remember one prayer I had in particular with God that went something along the lines of "I'm willing to die, if you would just save my mom."

One of my biggest fears was my mother going to hell. I was more afraid for my mother to go to hell and be alone, than I was about not making it to heaven. I was so wrapped up in getting her to love herself the way I did, that I stopped caring about myself.

I always felt that when I grew, my mother should have too. I felt like my understanding of life and relationships and hers were the same. I don't anymore though. I see now that we all grow at different paces, and what may have seemed like hell for me could have been smooth sailing for another individual. The problem was not my mother or her sexuality, it was my expectations of her. Disappointment can only thrive where there is expectation. I compared our demented relationship to the ones of everyone around us. I compared and contrasted my way into being depressed. I realized there was no amount of faith I could put in her that would make her change into the perfect woman I'd dreamt of. That was God's job. I couldn't even hear what He was directing me to do because I wanted share any bit of deliverance I got with my mother…but it doesn't work like that. Have you ever heard of the women that die saying the same ole' "save my husband, brother and cousin" prayer? There's a season for that, and it shouldn't hold back your personal progression or consume your entire life. Eventually who you are, in God, wont be able tolerate any of foolishness you could once stand. This doesn't mean you love them any less, just gotta switch up the scenery in your life so you can breathe better. It was either take care of myself, or lose myself.

Today I couldn't be more proud of the woman my mother is. She's taking on rigorous coursework all while being the captain of a prison! Our relationships seems to get better by and by. She's an drummer at the church she attends and just awesome woman all around. She's so supportive of all of my efforts.

In retrospect, I see now that my mother did the best she could with the knowledge she had. She had given me everything she knew how to give and for that it's all love and will forever be.

When I started my junior year of college, I told my mother I wasn't sure where I would go, but living with her and the new woman she's involved with was out of the question. I've been through this before…a few times. I'll still be here when it all falls through too, I always am & with that mindset I rode the Cadillac she'd given me to Jackson Mississippi.

When I arrived at the school I hadn't applied for housing and I had a $3000 dollar balance. I didn't care though… I had never been more sure I made the right decision than then. I prayed before I got out of my car to enter the office of the apartments I live in now and I was confident I would walk out with something. One week into the semester my balance was paid, I lived in off-campus housing completely free, and I was later blessed with a job within those complexes. It's something about the activation of our faith that causes God to shift things on our behalf. I didn't care if I had to work two jobs in order to stay away from living with my mother and her partner, I would find a way. All those blessings happening consecutively was like God's way of telling me "it ion eem take all that", and I was glad it didn't!

Psalms 8:4-6

"What is man that You are mindful of him,and the son of man that You visit him? For You have made him a little lower than the angels, and You have crowned him with glory and honor. You have made him to have dominion over the works of Your hands;You have put all *things* under his feet."

Letter I found ripped from one of my old journal stuffed in one of my composition books…

" Jesus I know you love me but it seems like you hate me. I don't have a way to church and a lot of bad things have happened to us since we moved. I'm sorry for letting you down. Can you please tell my dad that me and my mom need him now? Everything was ok at first but now its not. Maybe she will want to be with him again. I just want a normal family. God please help us. If you hear me can you do something by next week? I'll do better in school and I'll pray more. p.s. could you help me get in contact with Jessie?"

I find it hilarious that I always tried to give God timeframes to do His work in when I was younger. It was always "in the next few days" or " sometime next month." A lot of times things we think are emergencies are really just tests of endurance. I've read so many stories about long suffering for the greater good. Stories like the one of Nelson Mandela, Job in the Bible, and all the participants in the civil rights movement from the 60's to the present remind me that ugly situations make for a great story. The question is: how many of us are willing to be the test dummies for fatherless homes, suffer wrongful imprisonment, torn relationships, and teenage pregnancies? Absolutely no one. That's why we don't get to choose. Before we were even in existence God knew every trial we would face, and whether you believe it or not…He prepared us accordingly. Until I began to be totally dependent on Him all I seen was the destruction from my past and not the beautiful testimony that would come from it. If you don't close this book understanding anything else, let it be this:

Your struggles were specifically designed to gain understanding about how to deal with the hardest parts of life. Nothing you've been through, or will go through will be wasted. Now that you have this knowledge, you have a new responsibility in the earth to share it with those who need it. It's all about advertising about who you *used* to be to attract those that are looking for a way out. From that – lives will be changed. We're all just searching for something or someone who is relatable and gets it…

In His Absence

Writing this book has forced me to reflect upon some of the unhealthy decisions I made knowingly. I understood the wrongness of my actions but not why I was continually attracted to the same bad situations. It was then that I realized that going so long without any father figure present had weighed more heavily on my adulthood than I'd thought. I only wanted men that were not available to me…like my father had been. Without the mentorship and lessons only a man could give, I tripped more times than I could count. After so many broken promises from him, I'd acquired a complex about anyone saying anything to me and not following through with it. I could do it, but people couldn't dare do it to me…

I was always trying to prove my worthiness to people who seemed to have everything all figured out. I was on a quest to find that one individual who understood why I needed them to keep their word. Back then, I valued words and actions at the same rate. Now, the only thing that counts is what people show me.

My father has never been in my life. I cried after having to write my previous sentence. I'm crying because I don't understand how in the world my heart held so much love for a man that I can only remember seeing 6 times. (I kept track in my journals) The last time I seen him I was seven. I'm twenty now. I used to hate him. I used to want to yell at the top of my lungs, "HOW COULD YOU LEAVE ME? WHY DON'T WANT YOU WANT ME? WHY DON'T YOU CALL ME? ME AND MOM NEED YOU!" (and the hardest question of them all) why don't you love me back? I loved him so much…I believed every promise he ever made me. No matter what my mother said about my father in his absence I was there defending him. She didn't speak of him too often besides when he was behind on child support. I had his back every time and he never had mine.

Those six times I seen him I held on tight to what he looked like, how he smelled, and how he told he me he loved me a thousand times because he knew his next visit wouldn't be soon. I tried not to ask my mom about him too much because I didn't want to hurt her feelings more than he already had. His absence broke my heart a thousand times, and I still wanted him to be a part of my life. I'm not sure under what circumstances my mother and my father met, I'm guessing it was young love that ended just as quickly as it began. I honestly don't care to know *all* the details, I mean who does? Right now…I just thank God I'm here.

The resentment I held for my father was intensified by the situation with my mother. It seems like so many black children have accepted the fact their fathers won't be around as the norm. I know after a while I did. It's like the lyrics in Drakes song "Look What You've Done" he says "boo-hoo, sad story, black American dad story." It's almost a "just get over it" spirit we're supposed to carry about never interacting with one of the people who created us. To my knowledge I have six brothers and sisters, and I've only ever met two. I could literally be walking down the street and over look one of my siblings.

The people I grew up with in Wisconsin weren't blood family either. They never treated me any different, but still, it would've been beneficial to know my real family. I've always felt misplaced when it came to the "family" aspect. Not only do I not know my father's people, but because my mother has a different father from the rest of her siblings, I've never met any of my family on that side either. I don't know what any of my aunts, uncles or cousins look like on my father's side and on half of my mother's side. They all live in New York, Wisconsin, or somewhere up north and that's pretty much all I know. The people in Tennessee are blood, but we hardly do anything together. It's like I'm a bastard on all sides and I guess that's why my sense of what family should be is little distorted.

I could waste time being upset for no one assuming the responsibility early on to make sure I knew who my family was, or I could get out there a do it myself. I've chosen the latter. I've been trying to hawk down cousins and aunts on my mothers side via Facebook and asking my father about the names of my cousins on his side and what my grandmother was like. I'm currently trying to set up a trip to meet my little brothers and sisters so that they'll know who I am, and that big sis loves them. All of my efforts are about taking responsibility for the way I want my life to be. Not where it is now, but where it will be by the time I'm finished doing everything in my might to turn all that is ugly, beautiful.

I don't want you to die angry with anyone…okay? Stop focusing on what could've been done or who should've been there and accept the reality that you were wronged and no one can go back in time and fix that. Own your truth. Your truth is all the ugly things you try and hide about yourself and your family. Until you acknowledge the things you want to change, you wont have any idea where to start. If there is anyone you've cut off because of who they used to be, or what they used to do…forgive them. You owe it to yourself to live as peaceful, and whole as you can.

I had to get to a point where I refused to grow old and bitter. I realized that as long as my father is alive we have a chance to start over! How many great people have you blocked out of your life because you only acknowledge them by who they *used* to be? Everyone is so afraid of giving second chances like God hasn't given us thousands. Unforgiveness in our hearts will rot existing relationships. Although there may be a new person in the picture, your pain will only allow you to expect the worse out of them because of what you've already experienced. Heal before you go around establishing new relationships with people, or you could end up being the very person you've been trying to avoid.

Recently my relationship with my father has improved. We call and text each other here and there and I'm honestly so impressed with the man he's become. He's on the path to become an ordained minister and works at a local women and children's abuse center in Los, Angeles. You know you've forgiven someone when you don't care where they are or what they do just as long as their life is better because of it. I couldn't let my feelings continue to manipulate me into being upset from things that happened so long ago. I finally learned how to water only what can grow upright in my life and starve the rest.

Thought Provoking Moment

What seeds have you been watering in your life? What weeds have you let take over healthy crop because you were too lazy to pull them up? On a piece of paper write down the names of the people who water you…and the people who are only watching to see if you will fail or not. Who do you hang around that inspires growth?

I've moved on but I will never forget the sting of not being taught valuable lessons about men early on, or how it felt to miss and think about a man who could care less about me. I can't forget because I perpetuated that with every man I involved myself with afterwards. I believe the absence of the head of the household can make everything that was supposed to be under him deteriorate.

The Honorable Mentions

Speaking of men, I guess I have a list of my own honorable mentions.

My first boyfriend was cute and we started dating my junior year of high school. He was cool, but he was also a pushover. I think I broke up with him like three times before he finally decided he didn't want to deal with my shenanigans anymore. I can't really say much about him because he was so routine and predictable. I don't remember him ever surprising me, there were virtually no plot twist with him. The only thing that was memorable was that I lost my virginity to this fellow, and I'd rather forget that entire awkward ordeal. We're still cool to this day. I was never in love with him but I did lie to him and tell him I was. I broke up with him about three times and it didn't hurt at all when he *finally* let me go.

The first guy I was in love with, and actually loved

me back, was my best friend of three years. He always had an amazing ear to listen to everything I was going through. We told each other it all, until we started to fall for each other. That ended pretty messily.

The second guy I really got involved with was a country boy my sophomore year of college. He wasn't all that when I first seen him. I was really at a place in my life where I just wanted more of God and success. I was in the midst of trying to figure out who in the world I was. Then here came his tale telling me how beautiful I was, paying for dates and whispering sweet nothings in my ear. I fell for it. I hate I did, cause babbbby I fell hard. I was stupid, mentally unstable in love with this guy. Either way we shared some pretty passionate moments in weird places that I will never forget. He taught me a lot about the way men operate. He was so stuck on being the perfect example of what a couple should be and he wanted me to join in on his fairytale. I was too ashamed to tell him I was far from perfect and had no intentions on acting like I was. We ended horribly and I was heartbroken. I literally threw rocks at his dorm room window at 3:00 a.m., wrote love letters, bought him stuff and text him a thousand times a day. That was crazy. I'm glad I got outta that.

This next guy is a different case. He was cool with his approach. I honestly fell for him before I even knew him. I think it was his image, and ability to be hot and cool at the same time. What I mean by that is the fact that he was in the public eye and admired by many, but also had another side to him that I had the privilege to know about that was a completely different persona. I jacked that up before I ever got the chance to really know him because…well let's just say his friend caught my eye too. Since then I've deleted his number to keep down the amount of times I randomly decide to text him (I'm still young, and still spontaneous). I'm not flattered by his looks…I mean he's handsome, but I think what I admire most is his ability to balance. I like stability although I never seem to have it until I'm all alone.

This last guy was my wildcard. I met him through a social media platform, and he was cool. Things escalated quickly between he and I. He lived about twelve hours away so face time was our best friend until an opportunity came up for me to visit him. This is the first man in my entire life I completely ignored the looks department on. He was not attractive to me even dressed up. I had to close my eyes to kiss him. Nevertheless he was sweet, took me out to some nice spots and loved God. The only thing is, he was still butt hurt over his ex. He thought I couldn't tell…but I could. She was written all over his statements, and he even still wore the t-shirt she had made for her business. He's a pretty well known guy, and considerably older than myself. We would've never worked out though cause neither of us was feeling the other enough for various reasons. One of the things I can appreciate about him was his grind! He would wake up at 6 a.m., go to bed at 2 a.m. and wake up and do it all over again. We had some pretty interesting conversations. One thing that will always stick with me is him telling me to "never be anyone's slave", we were talking about it in the context of talented people working mundane, lifeless typical 9-5 jobs, but I took that and applied it to every part of my life.

Of course there were plenty of "in-betweeners" who were pretty pointless… besides to fill up empty time. I got played a few times, and done a little playing myself. I had to get hip to how men operate early in the dating game, because I'm not built like the average twenty year old. That's not me be being cocky either, that's just the reality of the situation. I've "talked" to men ranging from a multi-million dollar lawyer, to a local dough boy. I think what I was attracted to the most was power. It was like an elixir that burned in my veins. It was nothing like people who could have almost anybody they wanted, choosing you. I used to be silly and think it was because of how awesome of a person I was. Now, I know that most of the time it was based on physical attraction and that alone. I'm not air headed enough to appease only that aspect for a man though, eventually I'm going to have to open my mouth and pick at the brain I'm considering getting to know. I've never been interested in surface level conversations. I guess I've never been interested in men who actually liked me for my mind either. That one stung…but hey, it's true. Enough about me and my love life… Gotta have a few failures to know when the real thing comes around, right?

I think the most valuable information I can tell young people when it comes to relationships, is that until someone makes a commitment (doesn't have to be marriage) but just some type of understanding of what you're around each other for, consider that person an ornament. Yes, decorations are pretty but we don't make life long commitments to stuff that's only supposed to be seen for a season. We pull 'em out for Christmas and Thanksgiving and then its time for them to go back in the box. It's not healthy to be looking for marriage and/or long commitments out of every person you meet that shows a little interest. Some are sent for friendships while others are just passing through to teach you a lesson. Don't attempt to secretly match-up everyone you meet to the scroll of qualifications you've written. Yes, the process of sorting 'em out will be fast paced but it will help free up so many unwanted, worrisome connections. Understand the law of mutuality…if the person wants what you want, it'll be obvious. Just be patient.

I don't live my life in fear of the next time I'll fail anymore. In fact I've gotten used to jumping in head first unconcerned with how deep the situation may actually get meaning, I'm not seeking deep soul connections with everyone I meet. I'm learning how to use discernment and make sure those I invite in have been tried over and over again before they get the privilege of my time and energy. Those two are precious.

These are lessons I had to learn myself, they weren't passed down to me through my mother or by an overprotective father, but just by me feeling my way through the world. No one wants to wake up and listen to your dreams and about how much you want to please God after you've already given yourself away.

I'd Met Him Before 08/29/14

Familiarity. I remembered
those same lines being
spoken to me before just
rearranged and from a
different voice. I always
moved about as if the pain
from the last one didn't
matter. I was far too
transfixed on attempting to
get a hit of the antidote so
many choose to consume,
before sickness ever enters
their members. I had
rearranged my priorities and
ensured the phone was close
so I couldn't miss your
beckon. The opportunities
to chill meant he seen my
beautiful potential? It meant
he seen I loved God, art,
literature and music right?
To be handpicked by this
type of man must have meant
something. He had to have

known I was different.

Not just cliché different either…but a genuine encounter with a rare being. I moved different, and I was prepared to open him up to the beautiful world inside of myself that I rarely ever got to share. I was willing to share all my insecurities with him and provide a place for him to hide his in me. I'd be his secret keeper, his chef, his lover, his down chick and comforter…I just needed some

attention.

The ones that keep me waiting always kept my attention longer than the ones that blew me up. I was used to waiting on pins and needles for the one

experience to show him all
that I was…but there was
never enough time

He had already reduced me
to a piece of ass. So like a
dealer, I let him test drive this
vehicle.

& like all drifters do he was
never able to reciprocate any
of the vibes I was throwing.
See the joke was always on
me…it was all a "just in the
mean time" typa attraction.
He had already become
adjusted to detaching any
emotional value that sex
carried…and I cant believe I
didn't see it coming…

I could've sworn I'd met him
before.

Just be Yourself (that's enough, I promise)

Some things you just can't teach. Some things only come by way of experience. I think social media has tainted the mind of today's men and women. Subconsciously we believe we need to live up to the quotes perpetuated down our timelines.

As I said before…it's all a matter of learning how to navigate through life. You gotta discard the game players for the ones that haven't become so adjusted to Americanized standards of beauty and masculinity that they prefer you….just you, with no added preservatives, fake colors or flavors.

Why do we delete photo's that don't get enough "likes"? Why does our confidence depend upon what other people think? What is the beauty standard when a woman is praised for the courage it takes to wear the natural hair that grows out of her head? Why does it take courage to do that? Who made it *not* okay to be the way God created us? It's way too cool for our generation to not have feelings, to love'em and leave'em. We raising a generation of numb individuals and by the time it's time to actually feel something for someone…the trust factor is completely destroyed. You shouldn't have to exaggerate or downplay any part of your personality to get people to accept you. If you like to read, cool! That's you. Own the fact that you're a bookworm and don't dummify (yes, I just made that up) yourself to appease anyone who doesn't. I used to think I needed to be relatable to everyone I encountered, so I tried to pull out of myself whatever they were familiar with to spark a conversation. Being who people need you to be gets old…quick. A lot of people will recognize your light, but won't be able to handle the glare. The moral of the story is to be SO you, that you intimidate people who think changing people works. Only invite positivity, love and good vibes into your space.

In 2013 after attending a private predominately white Southern Baptist Christian school I started to get life, not completely…but I just started to understand where I fit in this whole equation. I was so used to shutting everyone out, and faking who I was to those who were close to me. Being at a school where I didn't know anyone gave me time to clear my head and finally focus on myself. I was able to start dreaming without limitations. At first my thought process was tied to the judgments I knew we be coming right after I made a decision. That's no way to live. In fact, it's slavery…once a person has your mind they have your actions, and your strength along with it. Everything you have ever done and will ever do starts with a thought. It's up to you whether or not you will become a slave to opinions.

Recently I went to see a movie entitled "Beyond the Lights" and it was about a young woman who had lived her entire life for other people. Her every move was directed by her *mom*ager. It eventually got so heavy for her that she not only thought about suicide, but actually attempted to take her life all because no one had ever let her be herself. She wasn't the sultry lights, camera, action star her team wanted her to be. She lived someone else's life so long that it nearly killed her.

Don't be that person.

Make your own decisions. Follow your dreams even if they seem silly to everyone around you. Be your own cheerleader. Enjoy the silence of your own company while you're working on something for the world. Take out the time out to listen to your thoughts and put them into action. Half of the battle of following your dreams is believing you can do it. The other half is preparation. You gotta stay ready so you never have to get ready. Let learning about whatever it is your passionate about consume all of the free time you have. Eat, sleep, and breathe that thing. There are so many self-taught experts out there that have little to no formal education. Perfect your gifts. I know of so many musicians and artist who've never had any training in music or fine arts but still are just as talented and noticed. The question is... how does someone become good at something they've never been taught to do?

They grind. Most of the work you see in any profession is the result of hours upon hours of grinding behind the scenes. These are the people that don't make excuses like "I don't know how, or I don't have enough money." These are the people that try out every idea they have, write down more, and then try those. You can never be defeated if you don't consider anything you do a loss. You either win, or you learn…but you never lose.

Nothing worth having will come easy. If you

commit yourself to your vision, even through adversity, you'll be like a bulldozer. All that passion starts to drown out the negatives and it's like having tunnel vision. Every failure is only an opportunity to learn where we went wrong, correct it, and try once more. I think Steve Jobs explained it more eloquently than I ever could. He said, "If you are working on something you really care about, you don't have to be pushed. The vision pulls you." For myself, this is absolutely true. When I'm working on writing, painting, or preparation to speak somewhere I can't sleep because of all the ideas bouncing around in my head.

It's important to remember that no one will support your work anymore than you do yourself. Why should they believe in something you don't even think is possible? All types of pressures will come when you are working on something that you can uniquely call your own. Don't be tempted to intertwine your purpose with anyone else's. There will be people who see where you're headed and have absolutely nothing to contribute to the process. Those types are only in it for the ride to your success. People will resent you for choosing change. Just be prepared to set your mind to "airplane mode" when it comes to all the distractions that will arise. Let your ear be sensitive to what the Creator is saying for your life. Don't feel like a fool following your dreams, you are not the only person putting it all on the line – trust me.

Abortions 9/16/14

We are sometimes molested
by those closest to us. Not
physically restrained, but
forcibly penetrated with
negativity, hurt and botched
realities of what life should
be. Beware of those who are
naked and offer you
clothing. Those are the ones
willing infect you with
dangerous rhetoric until
your identity is simultaneous
to that of their own. Cut the
umbilical cord that feeds
every seed they planted. End
the dialogue with people
who always feel the need to
deter you from your
purpose. If you choose to
birth their ideas with
chromosomes missing no

one but you will be
responsible. There is no
insurance policy for the
retardation that will ensue.

Lie down…

open your mental legs…

& rip away all that stunts
your growth.

Love…The World Most Durable Power

So after I'd gotten used to ignoring the weight of acknowledging everyone else's opinions, I had to re-learn how to think for myself. I made some really horrible decisions in that process. I'd mistaken the liberation of my mind for rebellion. I challenged everything… even the things I already knew were beneficial for me. I was so lost and running wild from people that I forgot the entire point of me realizing who I was, was in order to help others find themselves. Maya Angelou has a quote that says "when you get, give and when you learn, teach." I'll never forget hearing her say that…I took it literal. Nothing that I've learned or acquired is my own but all for the sake of the greater good of humanity. It's hard being a constant giver because, sometimes, when it's time to get your batteries recharged there's no one around to help you with that. Still, you have to be persistent with what you know to be right and true. I've learned that the only way to be who I am in spite of those who will attempt to take advantage of me is through love.

The problem is that I'm so used to seeing artificial love. You know, Instagram love? The kind of love that needs an audience to stay relevant. One of my favorite humans, Martin Luther King Jr., believed that love was "the most durable power in the world". I went through a phase where I was obsessed with this man and his speeches, prolific essays, and sermons so when I say I love him and I know his work, it's probably an understatement.

In a sermon from 1956 he was trying to warn people about all the things that would rise against them for standing for something, which at the time was the bus boycotts. He told them, "I still believe that standing up for the truth in God is the greatest thing in the world. This is the end of life. The end of life is not to be happy. The end of life is not to achieve pleasure and avoid pain. The end of life is to do the will of God, come what may. I still believe that love is the most durable power in the world."

All this time I was seeking attention, affection, and money and still none of those things made me consistently happy. In fact, nothing makes me happier than being able to give away love. Greek philosophers died searching for the "*summum bonum*" of life. What is the highest good one can do? Everything eventually fades. Materialistic gain, money, and beauty all have limitations and varying values but love's value never diminishes. I may wake up tomorrow and find that the value of the dollar has decreased but I will never have to wonder or worry about running out of love. It sounds cheesy, especially if you've gotten used to hatin' on people. Like many, I had gotten used to picking apart every little thing a person does, while begging for grace when it came to my wrongdoings. No one has room for error, when everybody chooses to be a critic. I had to get to a space where I just wanted to love people, regardless to how much money they had, where they came from, or how they looked, I wanted to love on folks. That is agape love. That is God's love for us.

The FBI considered MLK the most dangerous man in the world at one point. How so? Because no matter what people did to him or said about him he moved about with love. Government officials sent a letter to Dr. King trying to persuade him to take his life, bugged his phone calls, and lost a lawsuit against his family in which they were found guilty for killing him (google it) and he STILL wanted brotherhood. Personally, I haven't quite reached his level of agape"ness" but I understand better now how important it was to make sure love was a verb, and not just something he spoke about.

Martin would go and eat dinner with people he knew were badmouthing him as soon as he wasn't around. That's just the type of man he was. I always pictured him smoking a cigarette to calm his nerves and asking himself "what would Jesus do?" right before he made decisions. There's a story about Martin I heard Tavis Smiley talk about while speaking on his book over Martin's last few months entitled, "Death of a King." It was about Martin going out on the balcony of his hotel at about 3 o'clock in the morning. Everyone that was lodging with him were in a panic because no one could find him. When they finally found him, he was quietly singing an old hymn to himself. They tried speaking to him and asking him why he wasn't in bed and he wouldn't respond to anyone. They returned at about seven in the morning and there Martin was, still looking off into the distance singing that same old hymn. When I learned about this story I realized that brother Martin was operating out of something most people speak about but never embody…God's love. He had a intimate connection with the entity he spoke of so often. He was absolutely in love with God and in tune with His voice. This doesn't mean he didn't get scared, angry, lonely or sad like the rest of us, it just meant he had a stronger resolve to pick himself back up.

After studying him for a while I started to pick up on how he navigated through the vicious south without having a mental break down. Every move he made was one that would arise the sense of shame in his opponent without him having to tell people what they'd done wrong. He loved people while they were throwing hot coffee on him. He loved people while they were beating the elderly right before his eyes. He loved people that bombed his communities churches and killed brown people everyday day. That's some of the most intricate planning I have ever seen. It's so easy to retaliate and be violent and to try and make people "pay" for what they've done to you…but you still haven't succeeded in changing their minds or hearts.

I've found that love in the face of adversity transforms people. It arises a set of questions in the oppressors that they must answer. It makes people question their humanity without you ever having to lift a finger.

Not even the fear of death will stop me from giving love, and standing in the gap for those who have been gravely injusticed around the world. I don't care who I have to inconvenience to get the job done. It doesn't matter if it's domestic abuse, police brutality or starving children… if it needs to be addressed I will fight on their behalf like they are my own family members. I believe that's part what I was put here to do, to be a voice for those who have been neglected. I stand at the cross roads of the church and societal injustices and soul rehabilitation. All of these are my business are absolutely interconnected. I'll stand beside anyone willing to help those in these miserable conditions on earth.

If only we could all love without limits…what a utopia of a world this would be.

1st Corinthians 13: 4-8

"**4** Love is patient, love is kind. It does not envy, it does not boast, it is not proud. **5** It is not rude, it is not self-seeking, it is not easily angered, it keeps no record of wrongs. **6** Love does not delight in evil but rejoices with the truth. **7** It always protects, always trusts, always hopes, always perseveres. **8** Love never fails. But where there are prophecies, they will cease; where there are tongues, they will be stilled; where there is knowledge, it will pass away."

1st Corinthians 13:13

"**13** And now these three remain: faith, hope and love. But the greatest of these is love."

Vain Love 4/17/13

We'd all like to think we
love others without
expectations of receiving it
at an equal or greater
volume form which it let
our beings but
the truth is…
We encourage ourselves to
stay away from individuals
who cannot replicate and
reciprocate the love we
give them.
What type of love is this
that's dependent upon only
what others can give? Who
will love those who have
nothing but their mangled
pieces to provide? Who
will love the broken
hearted? Who will love
those who don't believe in
the concept of love at all?
What type of deficiency in

your being has made you
think you have the capacity
to deduce love to your level
of understanding?
It's rare to find one who
will love no matter the
circumstance or condition.
Sometimes we get so
absorbed consuming and
digesting the love of others
that we forget to
R a d i a t e love in the
same manner. If you got it
to give, please do. The
universe needs it.

Horror Summer

I started working on myself first it came to love but then like a cancer my past resurfaced. I went through what call "Horror Summer." I felt like the children in the books *A Series of Unfortunate Events* in the summer of 2013. The phrase, "if it ain't one thing, it's another" was my motto. Here's the list of everything that went wrong over those 3 months…

<u>How my life was ruined in 2013</u>

- Wrecked my first car that I bought myself (it was a hoopty …but still)
- Got caught stealing in the mall
- Went to jail and the same day I found out my two younger cousins found my aunt dead
- Started to drink heavily
- My mother had to undergo surgery for a potentially cancerous tumor

- Got taken to jail for driving on a suspended license
- Grades started slipping
- Stopped attending church
- Depression kicked in HARD

When I got wind through a friend my mug shot was being sent around in a chain text, I was devastated. My aunt's death took priority over everything I felt, although it was hard trying to be there for my cousins as emotionally detached as I was. The only way I can explain how I felt was dream-like, it was like everything was happening around me and I was just in the middle of it all without any control. Again…I wanted to give up on life. I didn't understand where I went wrong, and I was too ashamed to ask anyone for help.

I see now. I was half-ass'n it. I only gave a part of myself to the vision. I wanted to be different and appear to be this changed person but only bad enough so people could see it. I was so caught up in trying to convince people I was a new, evolved person that I didn't work hard enough on becoming her. I was more worried about mending my broken

reputation than focusing on my character.
Don't do whatever your passionate about looking for a response out of people. Don't alter your work because you want to make a certain amount of money and want it to be more received. You can't go through the process of dream building and get validation from everyone in the same breath.

I'm at a place now where I am not so obsessed with pretending that I'm perfect, that I can't show you where His grace has carried me. There were times when I felt so undeserving of God's love that I decided not even the blessings He promised me were worth finishing the path. It was then, that he carried me.

Half-ass Ambitions 11/11/14

Often times we decide to
take on new task but lack
the energy and effort it
takes to stay consistent. We
make bold resolutions to
change only seeking
temporary praises from
seasonal friendships and
folks who altogether don't
care.
The distance between what
we want and what it takes
to get there is so great that
the furthest we venture
from our bubbles of
comfortability is to the
front porches of the
confines our mind hold us
in.

The battle is between who we are and who we're supposed to be.

There are no shortcuts when it comes to working toward your vision. The ill-prepared often leave the journey feeling uncompensated and with far too many injuries to ever return, and when they do….
it's half-heartedly.

We have all the rhetoric it takes to build a dream and sell it, but none of the faith and substance required to endure everything that will arise to destroy it.

We want the promise but only bad enough so the people around us can see us

with it. Only to validate
that we aren't merely
existing but actually
contributing….and for
those reasons alone we
never see the vision
manifest.
Until we become
indigenous with the place
of pressure from which
diamonds are created
we will always o n l y be
the soot and dirt that covers
them.

Good enough to see it but
never becoming who we
truly are. Living life with
the consequences of having
half-ass ambitions…

A Breath of Fresh Air

The beginning of the summer of 2014 was a continuation of the few horrible months I'd had prior. I didn't know until the last minute that my mother had moved out of our apartment into the home of her new girlfriend. In fact, I didn't even know the woman was her girlfriend until I asked her after about two weeks of living in her home. I felt like my mother had not considered me in any part of that decision. All of my belongings were locked away in a storage forty-five minutes from the house. By that point, I was so sick of her making the same decisions that I wanted nothing to do with her or the woman. I was just wondering how many times she had to hit her head to figure out that these types of situations always ended horribly for her.

This time around, I won't play house, I won't act happy to appease her, and if asked, I'll tell the absolute truth about how I feel. When the truth offends people it's interpreted as disrespect, but I still don't mind telling it. I just don't have the time or the energy to deal with another attitude, meet another set of siblings, or open my heart to another kid. That game has long been played out.

I want to clear up something before I move any further…

The issue between my mother and myself is not because she considers herself a gay woman. I honestly don't care what sexuality she chooses and I have nothing against those communities. The issue lies within the poisonous relationships I was forced to endure alongside her. Did she raise me to accept homosexuality? No. Not at all. Which is one of my biggest agitations with her. I was extremely confused as a child as to how she told me the right thing and blatantly did the other. You don't get integrity points for saying the right stuff. I believe that made ***her*** feel better, it was one of those "at least I tried" type things. In the end all that counts is what she showed me. Her words became less and less valuable to me because she couldn't resist temptation enough to practice what she preached…and after a while all I had to hold on to was a scripture. The only reason I dealt with my mother at all was because the bible told me to honor her. I tried to stay as far away from that house as I could for as long as possible this past summer. I was sleeping from couch to couch over friends houses all summer long and living out of the trunk of my 94' Cadillac Deville. I hated the thought of having to return to a house where I didn't even have a bed and where I had an imaginary room.

It was my room, but with my mother's bed room suit and clothes filling the drawers. Here I was again, four years down the line, living out of my bins in the backroom of yet another woman's home. I tried to explain my sentiments to my mother but I'm afraid she didn't quite understand. I remember her explaining to me how economical it was for us to stay with her and how few bills she had to pay and I ended up more frustrated than when I began speaking to her. It was always something about bills and money. I told her to keep it this time, she should be happy where she finds happiness, and I'll go where I find mine.

That emotional split was so necessary. I had to learn how to care and have love for my mother from a distance. I'm not saying she did everything wrong when it came to me, but my mind is honestly flooded with horrible memories. I was always physically taken care of, just not always cared for. Of course she and I have had some really amazing times together, but they were far and few between and I still feel like I really don't know her.

Regardless to what I say, I'm not sharing this information with you so you can villain"ize" my mother. She's not a bad woman. I'm telling you these things so you'll understand how to overcome a broken relationship and yet love a person throughout the storm. None of the stupid decisions I made on my own accord were her fault. I stole because I thought I needed those things. I drank because I hated my life. My grades slipped because I stopped caring about school and even through all of that she loved me.

So after coming home from my sophomore year of college to what seemed to be another episode of hell I decided to make God a few promises. I looked up and said "God, I'm tired. From here on out, I'm willing to do whatever you ask of me…I just want to hear your voice. I just need to know that it's YOU directing me and not something I'm doing through my own raggedy intentions. Look man, I know it aint gonna work my way. I tried and the results have been suckey. So you gon' HAVE to step in and say something." That's how I talk to God. I'm not real elaborate and fancy with Him cause I ain't got time and He got a few million other people on His line at any given moment. Out of all the prayers and conversations I had talking *at* Him I'd never took the time to wait for a response. I'd never sat still long enough for Him to give me directions.

After that prayer everything started to slowly fall into place for myself. I was just trying to focus on keeping my intentions pure in whatever I did. All I could think about was planning….I didn't know why I was compiling all my writings together, or looking up Kematics, deciphering the difference between the denominations in the Christian faith and trying to understand the different components to atheism….but there I was. I went and re-opened every race relations book I had. I was visiting official government websites to get the accurate statistics of the people I would be dealing with. I was studying those things on top of my school work and absolutely consumed with gaining more knowledge. I felt like Malcolm X when he was straining his eyes to read even after the guards shut off the lights in his small prison cell. I was *that* thirsty for information! Learning became my happy place.

Throughout it all I discovered that I'm not religious at all. I'm not traditional. I learned that being a "good" Christian entails me being available for people of all walks of life and that even in disagreement; I'm still obligated to love them. The killer cops, those in the government that refuse to vote on policies that would significantly change the lives of people I deal with everyday, those that talk negatively about me but speak to me…all that is covered by love. I have to love the rapist, the murderer and the thief as much as I do the pastor, the schoolteacher and the nurse. It took me eradicating as much hurt as I could out of my heart to get here. I either had to break down, or use my energy to become who I knew I was. It wasn't a matter of being a brand new person, but unbecoming the one tainted experiences helped shaped. I opened myself up to a variety of perspectives and started to mold my worldview according to my new experiences with people. I began to live. Took myself to dinner, and museums, and different attractions all alone. I began to appreciate the fact that I was alive. It still brings tears to my eyes when I think about where I could of ended up. Now whenever I get heavy and feel like it's all too much to bear, I remind myself of the thousands of people who didn't make it out of their cycle of depression. I'm reminded of my mentally challenged cousin who has nothing but a box spring to sleep on. I'm reminded of everyone who is still in the middle of the mess that life sometimes brings. That pushes away the demons that try to cripple me. Looking back makes me grateful I experienced so much so early on. Without the scars, and me trying out different remedies I wouldn't be able to tell you what kinda ointment to put on yours.

Thank You, but Goodbye 6/3/2014

Today I own all of it, and
intend on telling its story
entirely. There is no
specific encounter with it
that I can say was my first
and forgive me but I can't
remember the first time it
held me captive long
enough for me to transfer it
to another individual in
order to restore my own
stability.
Gradually it has eaten at my
heart, encrypting itself
deeper than the codes under
the ancient pyramids.
Its "catfished" me so many
times appearing to be one
thing and manifesting itself
as another. It engulfs me so
at times that it methodically
transforms to rage making

me demolish any feelings
or hearts that get in its way.
To those I've hurt along the
way
I apologize, I was hurting.
I was hurting so bad that I
could not envision the
concept of ever being
whole again. It beat me like
a case of domestic violence.
My system never built up
an immunity to this
deficiency and like any
disease my body's immune
system sent antibodies to
wrestle with it only to find
that its natural remedies
were
misplaced.
It disfigured my
countenance and how I
carried myself in public. I
wore a beautifully crafted
mask designed to confuse
onlookers and hell, even the

operator. You've pressured
me into doing so much that
wasn't even meant for me.
You called me by my first,
middle and last name and
you just
keep
on
sending for me.
I've toyed with the
delusional idea of falling in
love with you. & though
on-lookers couldn't
understand, I got addicted
to how it felt…turning
down anything and anyone
that wasn't you. The fear of
you increasing your
intensity was too much
pressure.

I still got the marks from
your shackles around my
ankles, the rope burn from
your noose around my

neck. I've tried praying you
away, ignoring you all
together and even listing all
of your atrocities to a
confident.
Nothing has worked.

I still remember like
yesterday the times you've
brought me to my knees
with situations so bad they
suffocated the words clean
out of my mouth.
but now I know….
Brokenness is necessary to
appreciate the good days.
hurt
you no longer have
dominion over me.
I know that my efforts to
avoid you are in vain but
never again will you remote
control me.
So thank you, but goodbye.
Thank you but goodbye

Thank you but goodbye.

Go find someone who's
searching for ya.

Today

I would be lying to you if I said I didn't still have challenges. I still get nervous that people won't like my work. I still have conflicts within myself about ministering to people while battling my own issues. There are times when I feel like no one on the entire planet can relate to me, and that's okay. When you begin to really act on your dreams all the people who have been only drifting through life will get confused and intimidated. People are so afraid to open up about their struggles because of the fear of public crucifixion. Holding everything in will eventually make you ill and you'll get tired of having one persona for the world, and a different in private.

My family is still in disarray. I still get urges to make stupid decisions, like any 20 year old. I still don't know where I'll spend the summer of 2015 but putting my confidence in God has really helped with my anxiety of the uncertain. I know everything will get better for you, and for myself. My story is still being written and I'm so glad I had the opportunity to share it with you. If you've made it this far, you've almost completed the entire book. I know books like this usually end with happy fairytale endings, but I could never get jiggy with a life that was that predictable. Just learn to love the "fall down+ figure it out = valuable lesson" equation and you'll be alright.

If you ever get to the point where you feel everything is closing in on you, write about it. I've included a few blank pages in this book for you to lose your mind, write to God (or your devine being) and whatever else it takes to get the clarity you need.

Tell those that hurt you and God how you got through it…see me and you are close friends now. You know all my buisness. I thought about you the whole way through this process and decided not to hide anything from you. I've prayed for you, yes you, a thousand times before you even knew who I was. If you're reading this, then everything I said was meant for you.

Whoever you are, and whatever you're doing….know that God loves you and I love you. The rubric for your life is already written, you just gotta figure out what bullet point your own and go from there. Please go get what's yours…it'll go to waste if you don't. Keep loving and evolving.

- Yours truly,

A'Kayla Harris

If you would like to be included in A'Kayla's monthly e-newsletter and stay up-to-date with events she'll be speaking at, helpful resources, and her philanthropic efforts please send an email to thehealingjourney2015@gmail.com and tell us about how this book blessed you!

Journal Entries/ Notes

www.ingramcontent.com/pod-product-compliance
Lightning Source LLC
Chambersburg PA
CBHW051837040426
42447CB00006B/580